Ute and Tilman Michalski

Wind Crafts

Ute and Tilman Michalski

Wind Crafts

Everyone calls me
Craftie because I
love to do crafts.

Games and crafts with
wind and water for
children 5 years and up

ᕈ CHILDRENS PRESS ®

CHICAGO

Translation by Mrs. Werner Lippmann and Mrs. Ruth Bookey

Library of Congress Cataloging-in-Publication Data

Michalski, Ute.
   [Wie der Wind geschwind.   English]
   Wind crafts / by Ute and Tilman Michalski.
      p.   cm.
   Translation of: Wie der Wind geschwind.
   Summary: Instructions for making a windmill, houseboat,
bathtub crocodile, and toys that move in the wind and water.
   ISBN 0-516-09258-8
   1. Toy making—Juvenile literature.   2. Whirligigs—Juvenile
literature. [1. Toy making. 2. Handicraft.] I. Michalski, Tilman.
TT174.M5313 1990
745.592—dc20
                                 89-49553
                                     CIP
                                     AC

Published in the United States in 1990 by Childrens Press®, Inc.,
5440 North Cumberland Avenue, Chicago, IL 60656.

Copyright© 1990, 1988 Ravensburger Buchverlag Otto Maier
GmbH, West Germany. Originally published in West Germany
under the title *Wie der Wind geschwind . . .*

*I'll show you how
to make all these crafts
and tell you what you
need to
make them.*

CONTENTS

I'm almost ready to start. I just need to pack my tools.

Ready? Let's get started.

CRAFTIE

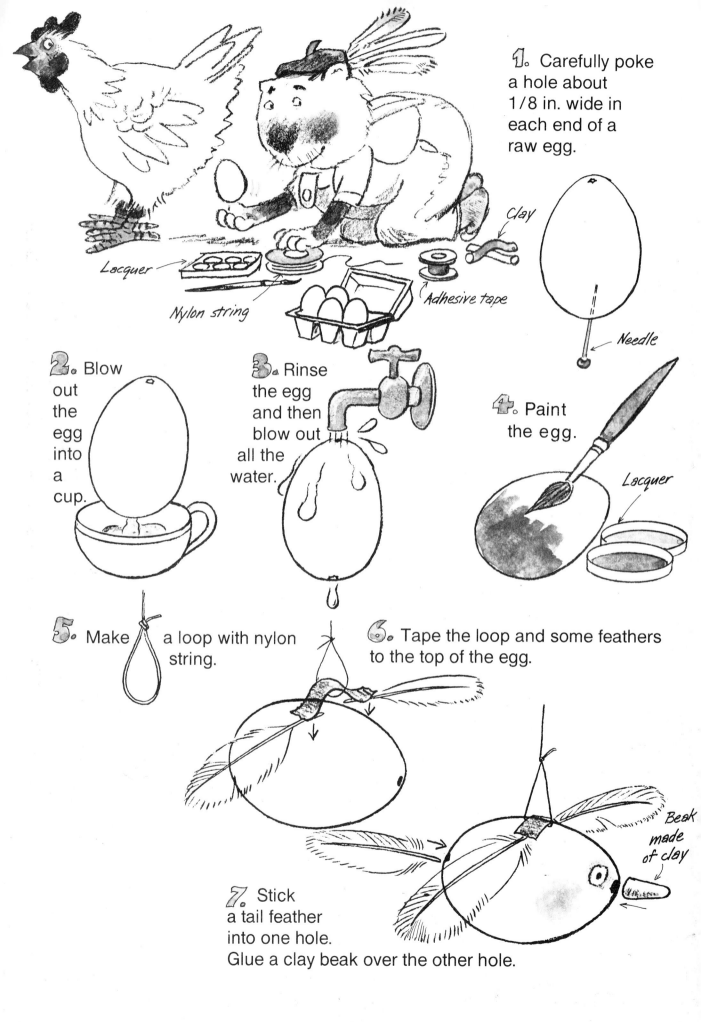

1. Carefully poke a hole about 1/8 in. wide in each end of a raw egg.

Lacquer

Nylon string

Clay

Adhesive tape

Needle

2. Blow out the egg into a cup.

3. Rinse the egg and then blow out all the water.

4. Paint the egg.

Lacquer

5. Make a loop with nylon string.

6. Tape the loop and some feathers to the top of the egg.

7. Stick a tail feather into one hole. Glue a clay beak over the other hole.

Beak made of clay

Flying Eggs

Emma, Fred, and Paula Bird try out
their wings in a flowering bush.
When will the berries be ripe?

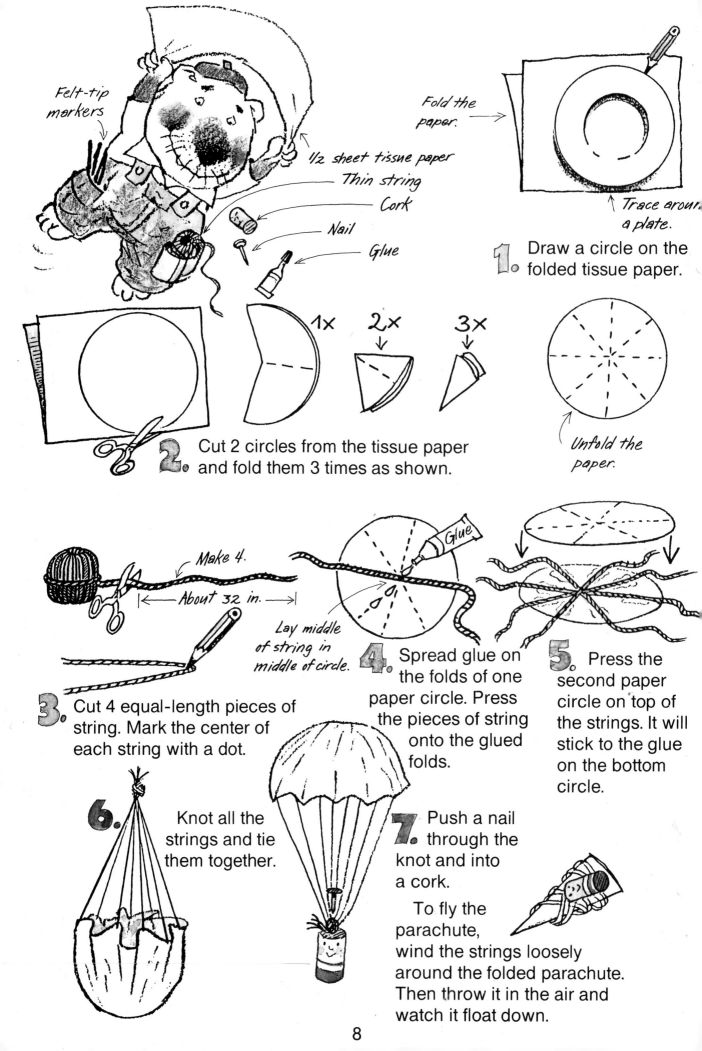

Felt-tip markers

½ sheet tissue paper
Thin string
Cork
Nail
Glue

Fold the paper.

Trace around a plate.

1. Draw a circle on the folded tissue paper.

1× 2× 3×

Unfold the paper.

2. Cut 2 circles from the tissue paper and fold them 3 times as shown.

Make 4.

About 32 in.

Lay middle of string in middle of circle.

3. Cut 4 equal-length pieces of string. Mark the center of each string with a dot.

Glue

4. Spread glue on the folds of one paper circle. Press the pieces of string onto the glued folds.

5. Press the second paper circle on top of the strings. It will stick to the glue on the bottom circle.

6. Knot all the strings and tie them together.

7. Push a nail through the knot and into a cork.

To fly the parachute, wind the strings loosely around the folded parachute. Then throw it in the air and watch it float down.

Sky Diver

There's big excitement in the
meadow when a cork sky diver
lands in the buttercups.

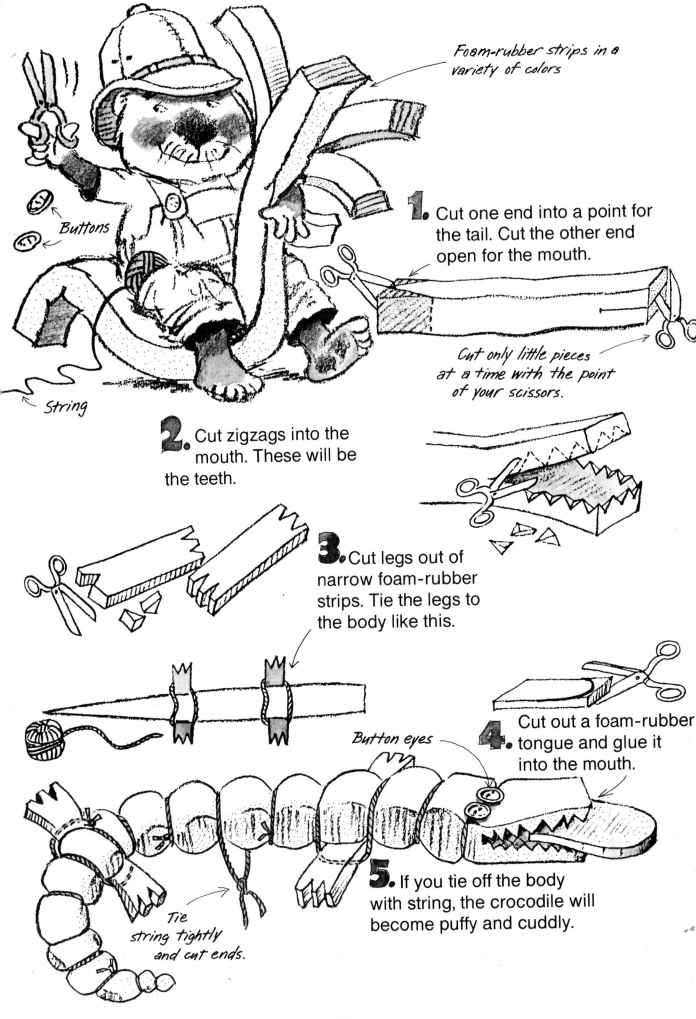

Foam-rubber strips in a variety of colors

Buttons

String

1. Cut one end into a point for the tail. Cut the other end open for the mouth.

Cut only little pieces at a time with the point of your scissors.

2. Cut zigzags into the mouth. These will be the teeth.

3. Cut legs out of narrow foam-rubber strips. Tie the legs to the body like this.

Button eyes

4. Cut out a foam-rubber tongue and glue it into the mouth.

Tie string tightly and cut ends.

5. If you tie off the body with string, the crocodile will become puffy and cuddly.

Bathtub Crocodile

Crocodiles are lurking
in the bubbles—waiting
to play with you!

thick wire

white and green paper strips of various lengths and widths

Long stick or dowel

Hole punch

Pliers

1. To make the wreath, fold two paper strips back and forth over each other. Always fold the bottom strip over the top one.

4 in.

2. Lengthen the wreath as needed by gluing on more paper strips.

Bend ends into hooks.

3. Punch a hole through the middle of the folded paper.

4. Thread wire through the holes and hook the ends together.

5. How to make decorations for the wreath:

Windball
1. Cut 2 paper circles and cut a slit halfway into each circle. Slide slots into each other.

2. Cut the circles as shown.

3. Fold back top halves of circles and slide 3rd circle over the folds.

Fold and push through.

4. Fold halves back as shown.

Fan Flowers

Paint colored stripes.

Watercolors

Fold.

Cut nick for string.

Glue.

Glue together.

Wind Bell

Cut here.

2. Slide two parts together at the slits.

3. Cut small green circles. Cut cross in center and stick onto stem of flower.

1. Cut 2 flowers.

Cotton ball

Birthday Tree

When the breezes blow, your flowers and bells will sway, and the wreath will turn in the wind. This tree will bring good luck if you "plant" it for your birthday or for a summer holiday.

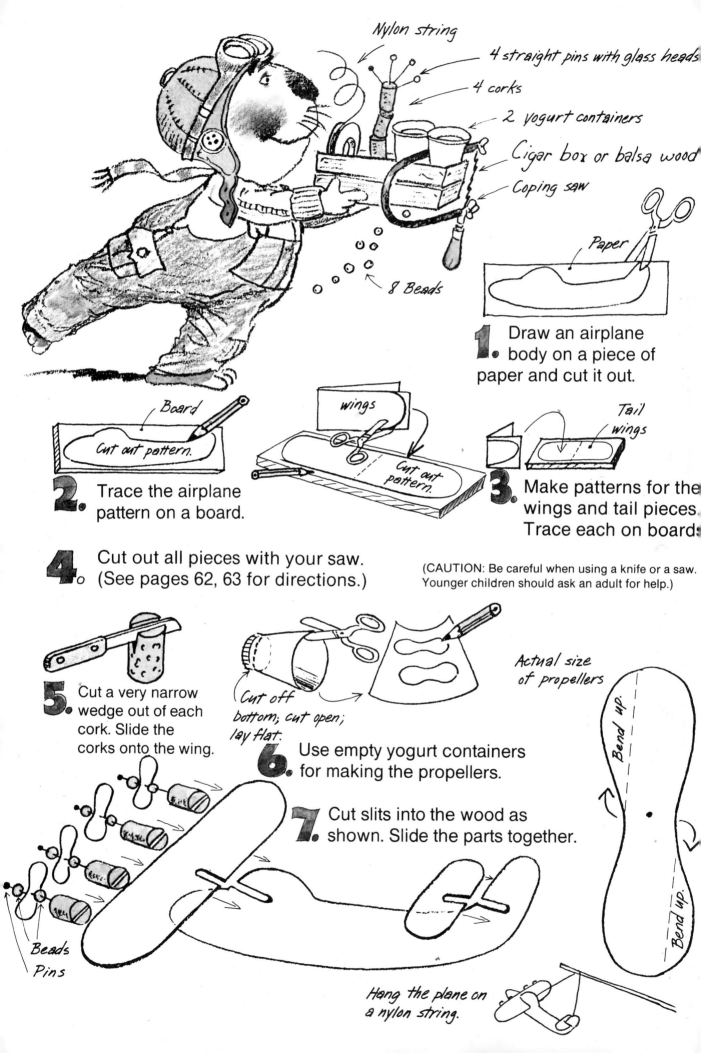

Nylon string

4 straight pins with glass heads

4 corks

2 yogurt containers

Cigar box or balsa wood

Coping saw

8 Beads

Paper

1. Draw an airplane body on a piece of paper and cut it out.

Board

Cut out pattern.

2. Trace the airplane pattern on a board.

wings

Cut out pattern.

Tail wings

3. Make patterns for the wings and tail pieces. Trace each on boards.

4. Cut out all pieces with your saw. (See pages 62, 63 for directions.)

(CAUTION: Be careful when using a knife or a saw. Younger children should ask an adult for help.)

5. Cut a very narrow wedge out of each cork. Slide the corks onto the wing.

Cut off bottom; cut open; lay flat.

6. Use empty yogurt containers for making the propellers.

Actual size of propellers

Bend up.

Bend up.

Bend up.

7. Cut slits into the wood as shown. Slide the parts together.

Beads
Pins

Hang the plane on a nylon string.

Flying Circus

Daring pilots show
their skill in the air.

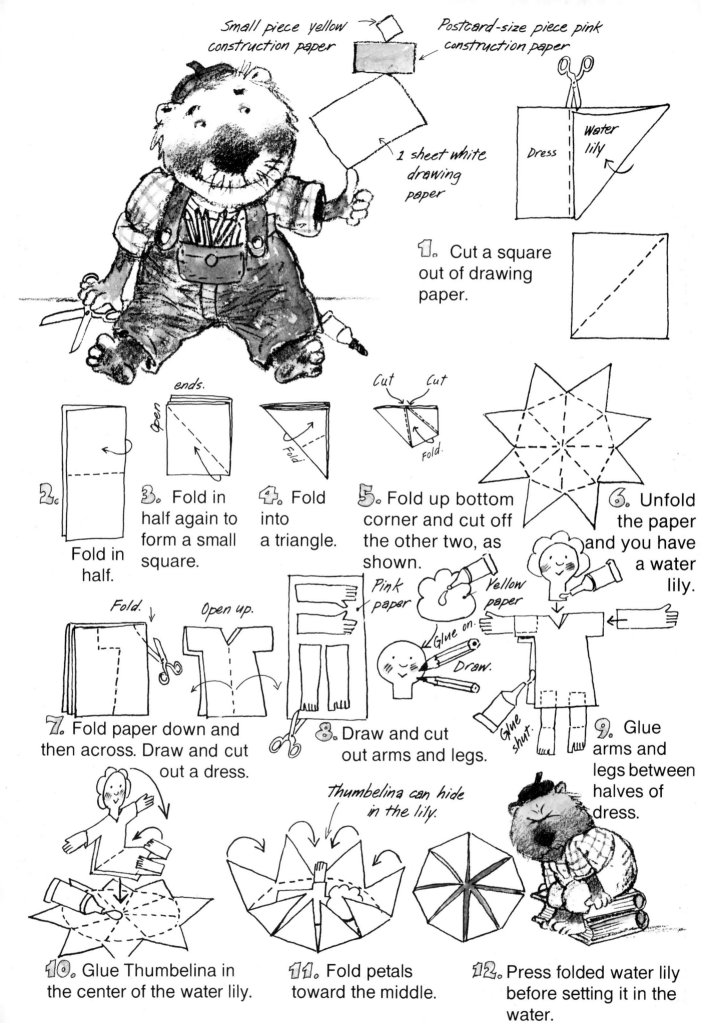

Small piece yellow construction paper

Postcard-size piece pink construction paper

1 sheet white drawing paper

Dress   Water lily

1. Cut a square out of drawing paper.

Open   ends.

2. Fold in half.

3. Fold in half again to form a small square.

4. Fold into a triangle.

Fold

Cut   Cut

Fold.

5. Fold up bottom corner and cut off the other two, as shown.

6. Unfold the paper and you have a water lily.

Fold.   Open up.

7. Fold paper down and then across. Draw and cut out a dress.

Pink paper   Yellow paper

Glue on.   Draw.

Glue shut.

8. Draw and cut out arms and legs.

9. Glue arms and legs between halves of dress.

10. Glue Thumbelina in the center of the water lily.

Thumbelina can hide in the lily.

11. Fold petals toward the middle.

12. Press folded water lily before setting it in the water.

16

Thumbelina

The water lily opens up in
the sunlight. Inside sits a
small girl. She's smiling.

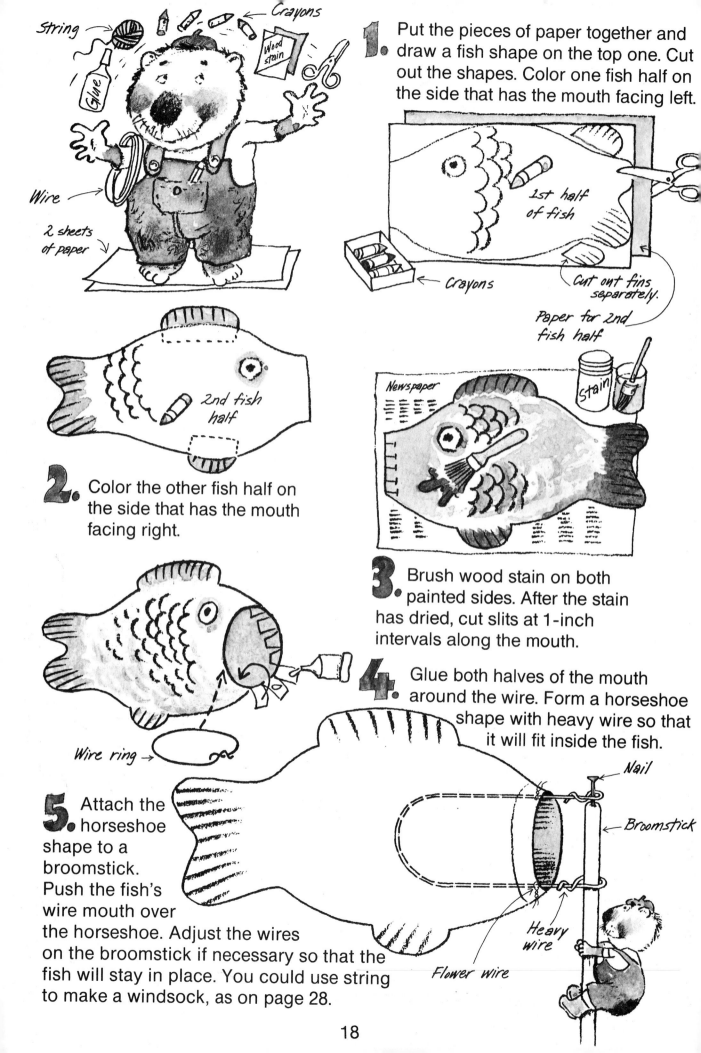

1. Put the pieces of paper together and draw a fish shape on the top one. Cut out the shapes. Color one fish half on the side that has the mouth facing left.

String

Crayons

Wood stain

Glue

Wire

2 sheets of paper

1st half of fish

Crayons

Cut out fins separately.

Paper for 2nd fish half

2nd fish half

2. Color the other fish half on the side that has the mouth facing right.

Newspaper

Stain

3. Brush wood stain on both painted sides. After the stain has dried, cut slits at 1-inch intervals along the mouth.

4. Glue both halves of the mouth around the wire. Form a horseshoe shape with heavy wire so that it will fit inside the fish.

Wire ring →

5. Attach the horseshoe shape to a broomstick. Push the fish's wire mouth over the horseshoe. Adjust the wires on the broomstick if necessary so that the fish will stay in place. You could use string to make a windsock, as on page 28.

Nail

Broomstick

Heavy wire

Flower wire

Flying Fish

It waves its tail and
swims through the air. Its large
mouth snaps at the wind.

Beech-nut shell

2 single maple-tree seeds for wings

6 thin, stiff pieces of straw

Chewing gum

2 leaves for wings

Cork

6 flat pieces of bark

1. Make the legs of the Water Walkers out of six pieces of straw of equal length.

2. Cut the bark into small, equal-size pieces.

You can use cork instead of bark.

(CAUTION: Be careful when using a knife, or have an adult do the cutting for you.)

3. Poke 6 holes into the cork for the straws.

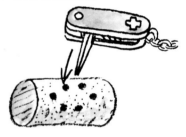

4. Spread the legs out evenly in a circle and stick them into small balls of chewing gum that have been placed on the bark pieces.

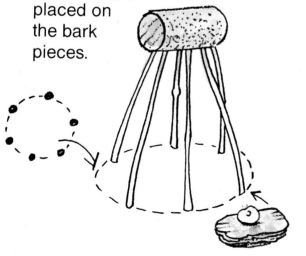

5. Use chewing gum to attach the wings and a beech-nut head.

Water Walkers

As the Water Walker moves over
the quiet waters, it occasionally
rests on the lily pads.

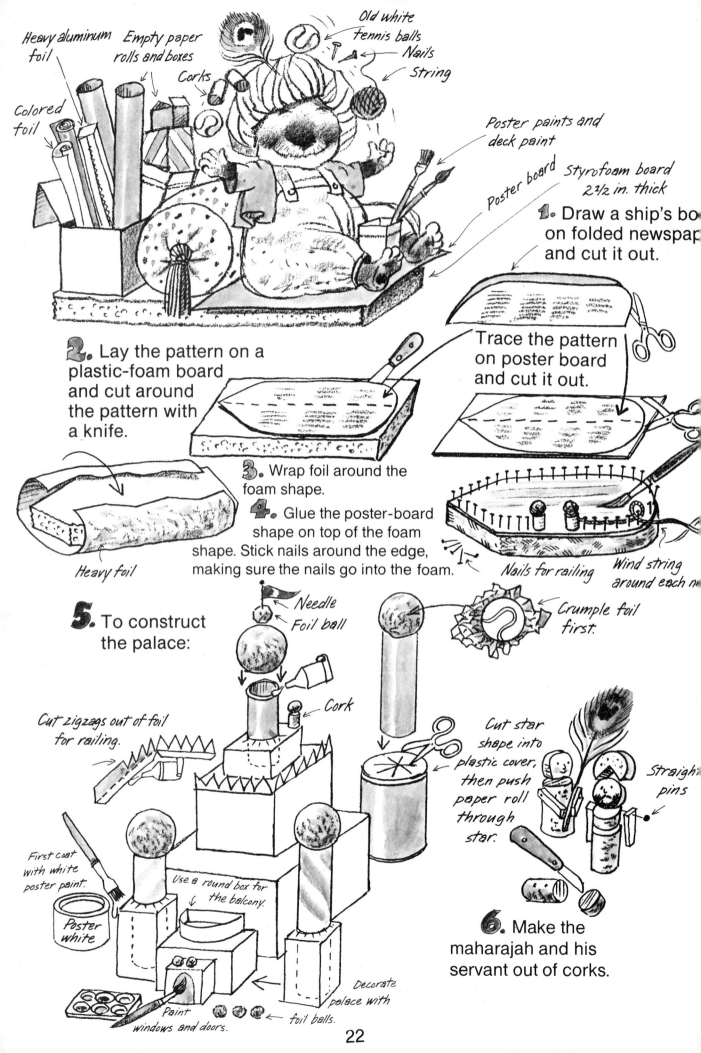

Heavy aluminum foil

Empty paper rolls and boxes

Corks

Colored foil

Old white tennis balls

Nails

String

Poster paints and deck paint

Poster board

Styrofoam board 2½ in. thick

1. Draw a ship's bo□ on folded newspap□ and cut it out.

Trace the pattern on poster board and cut it out.

2. Lay the pattern on a plastic-foam board and cut around the pattern with a knife.

Heavy foil

3. Wrap foil around the foam shape.

4. Glue the poster-board shape on top of the foam shape. Stick nails around the edge, making sure the nails go into the foam.

Nails for railing

Wind string around each n□

5. To construct the palace:

Needle

Foil ball

Crumple foil first.

Cork

Cut zigzags out of foil for railing.

Cut star shape into plastic cover, then push paper roll through star.

Straigh□ pins

First coat with white poster paint.

Poster white

Use a round box for the balcony.

6. Make the maharajah and his servant out of corks.

Paint windows and doors.

Decorate palace with

foil balls.

Floating Palace

The floating palace glides quietly down
the river through the jungle. This luxury ship
passes by water lilies and bathing elephants.

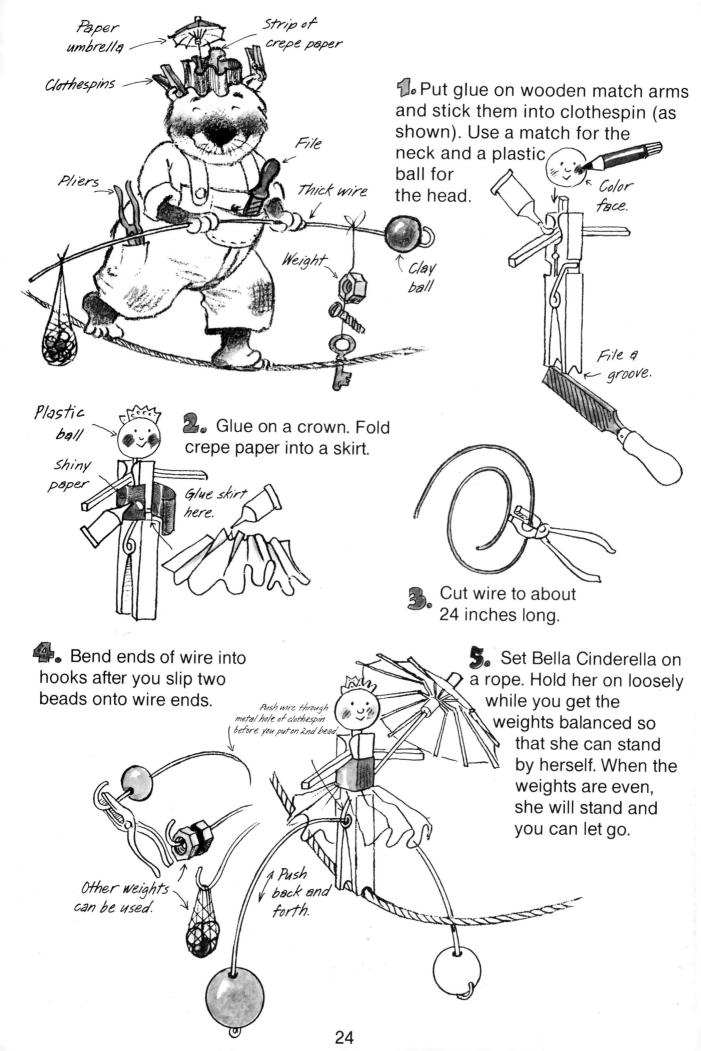

Paper umbrella

Strip of crepe paper

Clothespins

File

Pliers

Thick wire

Weight

Clay ball

1. Put glue on wooden match arms and stick them into clothespin (as shown). Use a match for the neck and a plastic ball for the head.

Color face.

File a groove.

Plastic ball

Shiny paper

2. Glue on a crown. Fold crepe paper into a skirt.

Glue skirt here.

3. Cut wire to about 24 inches long.

4. Bend ends of wire into hooks after you slip two beads onto wire ends.

Push wire through metal hole of clothespin before you put on 2nd bead.

Other weights can be used.

Push back and forth.

5. Set Bella Cinderella on a rope. Hold her on loosely while you get the weights balanced so that she can stand by herself. When the weights are even, she will stand and you can let go.

24

Bella Cinderella

The star of the clothespin
circus balances beautifully
on the laundry line.

Aluminum foil

Clear tape

Milk carton

1. Rinse out the milk cartons and cut off the tops.

2. Design and cut out different-shaped roofs and windows.

3. This is the way to lengthen the tower.

1st carton

2nd carton

Stick it together with clear tape.

Cut an opening into the back of each carton for the light.

Cut windows through foil and fold excess into center of carton.

4. Cover cartons with foil.

5. Tape the houses and towers together. Then tape them to a group of cartons that have been covered with foil. Set the castle to float in water.

Put small flashlights inside to light up the castle.

Aluminum foil

Clear tape

26

Water Castle

The castle is lit up. You are invited
to a frog concert followed by
a dance on the water.

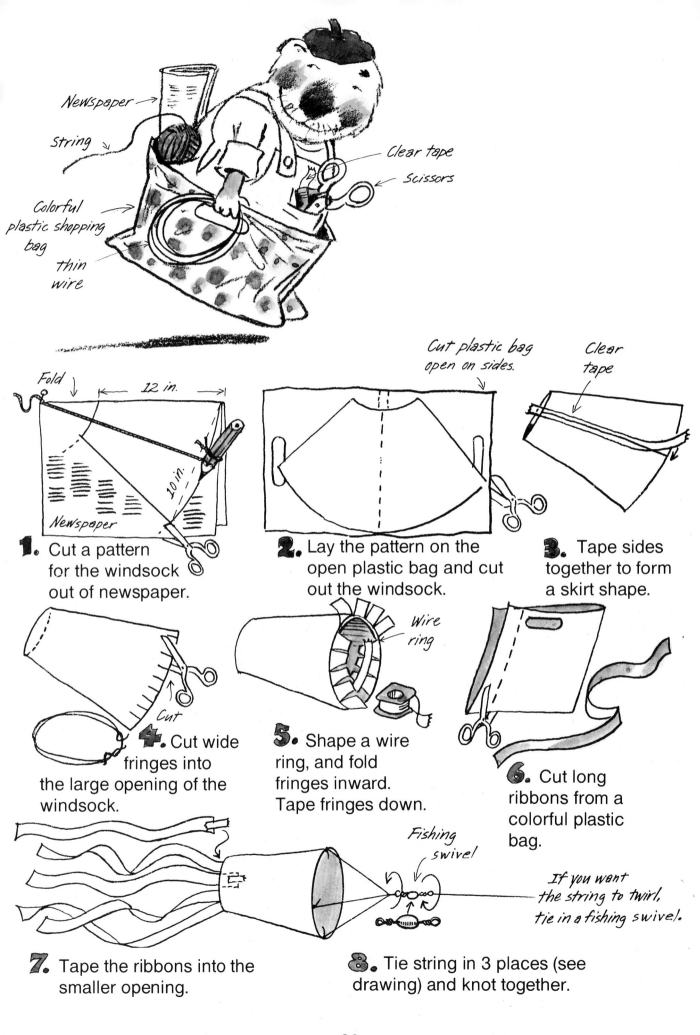

Newspaper

String

Clear tape

Scissors

Colorful plastic shopping bag

thin wire

1. Cut a pattern for the windsock out of newspaper.

Fold

12 in.

10 in.

Newspaper

Cut plastic bag open on sides.

2. Lay the pattern on the open plastic bag and cut out the windsock.

Clear tape

3. Tape sides together to form a skirt shape.

4. Cut wide fringes into the large opening of the windsock.

Cut

5. Shape a wire ring, and fold fringes inward. Tape fringes down.

Wire ring

6. Cut long ribbons from a colorful plastic bag.

7. Tape the ribbons into the smaller opening.

Fishing swivel

If you want the string to twirl, tie in a fishing swivel.

8. Tie string in 3 places (see drawing) and knot together.

Windsock

The windsock with its colored ribbons would look good attached to the back of a bike. The windsock will fly and twist as you ride along.

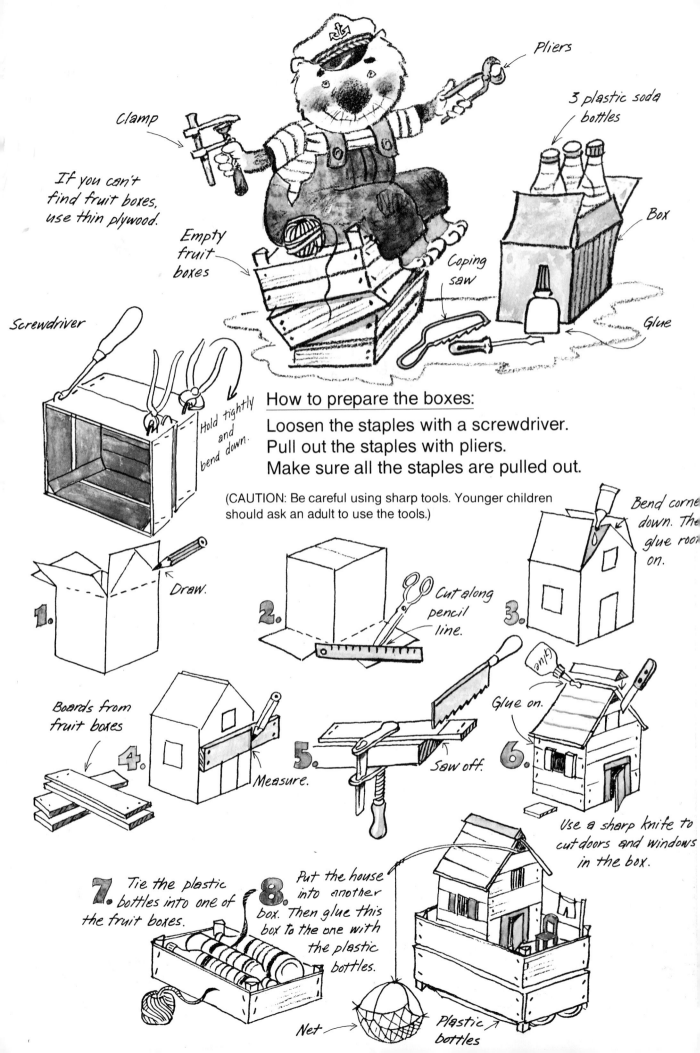

Pliers

Clamp

3 plastic soda bottles

If you can't find fruit boxes, use thin plywood.

Empty fruit boxes

Box

Coping saw

Glue

Screwdriver

Hold tightly and bend down.

How to prepare the boxes:

Loosen the staples with a screwdriver.
Pull out the staples with pliers.
Make sure all the staples are pulled out.

(CAUTION: Be careful using sharp tools. Younger children should ask an adult to use the tools.)

Bend corne down. The glue roo on.

1. Draw.

2. Cut along pencil line.

3.

Boards from fruit boxes

4. Measure.

5. Saw off.

Glue on.

6.

Use a sharp knife to cut doors and windows in the box.

7. Tie the plastic bottles into one of the fruit boxes.

8. Put the house into another box. Then glue this box to the one with the plastic bottles.

Net

Plastic bottles

Houseboat

The mice are going on a trip down
the Mississippi—as far as the
string will let their houseboat travel!

Chewing gum used for sticking things together

Reeds

Acorns
Wooden circle
Piece of cork
Leaf

Scale from pine cone

You can also make the head from a piece of cork or a horse chestnut.

Pine cone

Use as many natural materials as you can find to make the Indian. Whatever you happen to find can be put to use.

How to build the canoe:

1. Tie together three bundles of reeds.

2. Set the Indian into the middle bundle. Then tie the other bundles around it with the passenger securely tied into the middle of the canoe.

Secure Indian in center reed bundle.

Use bark as "floaters."

3. Push 2 sticks through the reeds and attach bark on either side to stabilize the canoe.

Chief Morning Wind

He sits near the shore of Spirit
Lake in his reed canoe,
waiting for a large fish.

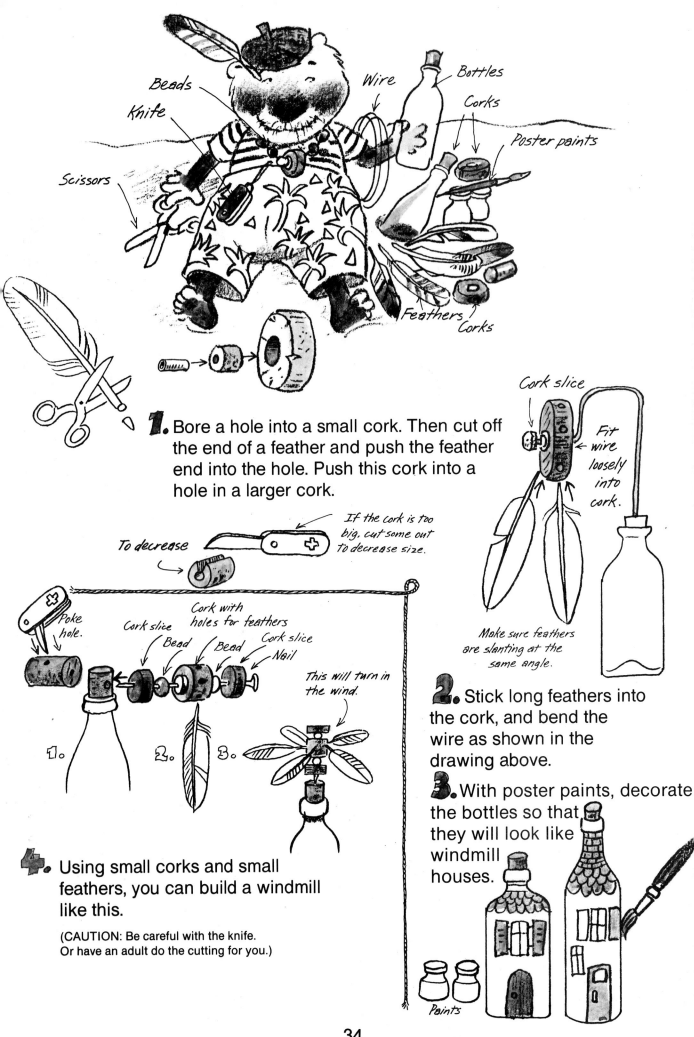

Beads

Knife

Wire

Bottles

Corks

Scissors

Poster paints

Feathers

Corks

Cork slice

Fit ← wire loosely into cork.

1. Bore a hole into a small cork. Then cut off the end of a feather and push the feather end into the hole. Push this cork into a hole in a larger cork.

If the cork is too big, cut some out to decrease size.

To decrease →

Make sure feathers are slanting at the same angle.

Poke hole.

Cork slice

Bead

Cork with holes for feathers

Bead

Cork slice

Nail

This will turn in the wind.

1. 2. 3.

2. Stick long feathers into the cork, and bend the wire as shown in the drawing above.

3. With poster paints, decorate the bottles so that they will look like windmill houses.

4. Using small corks and small feathers, you can build a windmill like this.

(CAUTION: Be careful with the knife. Or have an adult do the cutting for you.)

Paints

34

Beach Windmill

The sails of the windmills
turn in the wind, on
top of sand hills.

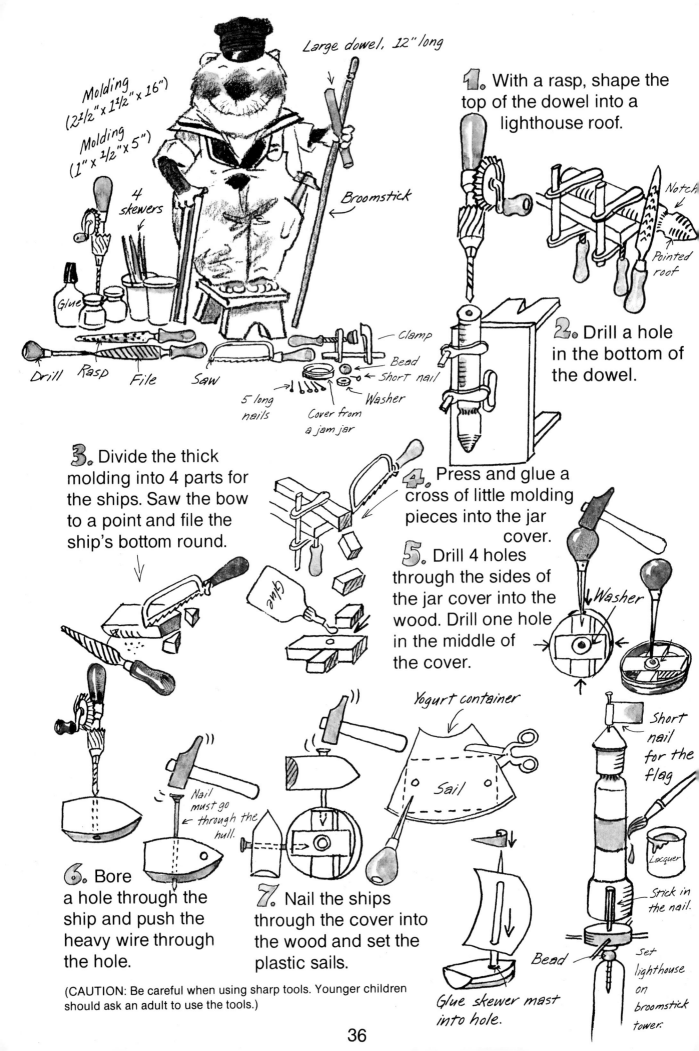

Molding
(2½" x 1½" x 16")

Molding
(1" x ½" x 5")

Large dowel, 12" long

4 skewers

Broomstick

Glue

Drill   Rasp   File   Saw

5 long nails

Cover from a jam jar

Clamp

Bead

Short nail

Washer

1. With a rasp, shape the top of the dowel into a lighthouse roof.

Notch

Pointed roof

2. Drill a hole in the bottom of the dowel.

3. Divide the thick molding into 4 parts for the ships. Saw the bow to a point and file the ship's bottom round.

4. Press and glue a cross of little molding pieces into the jar cover.

Glue

5. Drill 4 holes through the sides of the jar cover into the wood. Drill one hole in the middle of the cover.

Washer

Yogurt container

Sail

Short nail for the flag

Lacquer

Stick in the nail.

6. Bore a hole through the ship and push the heavy wire through the hole.

Nail must go through the hull.

7. Nail the ships through the cover into the wood and set the plastic sails.

(CAUTION: Be careful when using sharp tools. Younger children should ask an adult to use the tools.)

Glue skewer mast into hole.

Bead

Set lighthouse on broomstick tower.

Lighthouse

The wind is blowing the ships
around the lighthouse.

Glass pieces with dull-filed edges

Shells

Stones

Collect all kinds of little things from the beach, things that make sounds when the wind moves them and they touch.

Feathers →

Corks ↗

Pieces of wood and tree bark

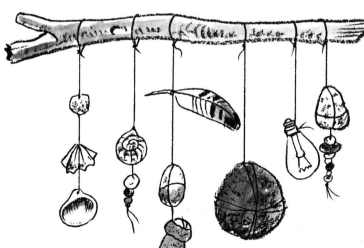

Tie all the pieces to a branch with string. Listen to the pieces as they knock together.

(CAUTION: Ask an adult to file the edges of the glass pieces for you.)

Beach Wind Chimes

Hear the soft tinkling sounds
as the chimes hit
each other in the wind.

Small piece of clear plastic wrap

5 plastic straws

Thin dowel

Crayons

Yogurt container

Colored cord

Rasp

Knife

Styrofoam

Tape

Plastic bag with a pattern

Styrofoam

1st half

2nd half

1. Both sides of the surfboard must be even so that it will float well. Make a model first.

2. Cut out the middle with a knife.

3. Roughen the underside a bit.

Thin dowel mast

4. Bore 3 holes and press the cap of a felt-tip marker into the front hole to hold the mast.

5. Cut a sail from a plastic bag.

Stick straws here.

Cut out a window and glue clear plastic over it.

Glue the sail around the mast.

Front

Hole

Hole

Pink

Little flag

Back

6. On the sail, paint a surfer the same color as the cord. Make two holes at the waist for the legs.

7. Thread the cord through the holes in the sail as shown in the drawing. Push the ends of the cord through the holes in the hull and tie knots at the ends. Do not pull the cord too tight. The legs should hang loosely.

Yogurt container

8. Glue a straw on the wind surfer's hands.

40

Wind Surfer

The surfer sails over the water
as fast as the wind!

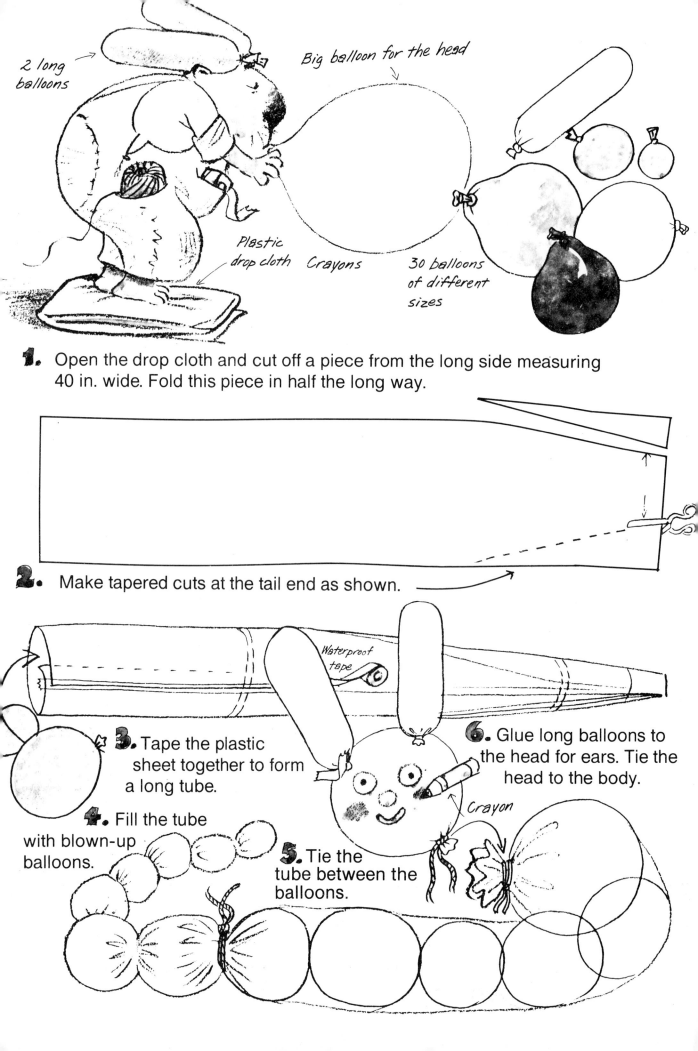

2 long balloons

Big balloon for the head

Plastic drop cloth   Crayons

30 balloons of different sizes

1. Open the drop cloth and cut off a piece from the long side measuring 40 in. wide. Fold this piece in half the long way.

2. Make tapered cuts at the tail end as shown.

Waterproof tape

3. Tape the plastic sheet together to form a long tube.

4. Fill the tube with blown-up balloons.

5. Tie the tube between the balloons.

6. Glue long balloons to the head for ears. Tie the head to the body.

Crayon

Water Snake

Some of the little children
are afraid of this monster.
Hear them squeal!

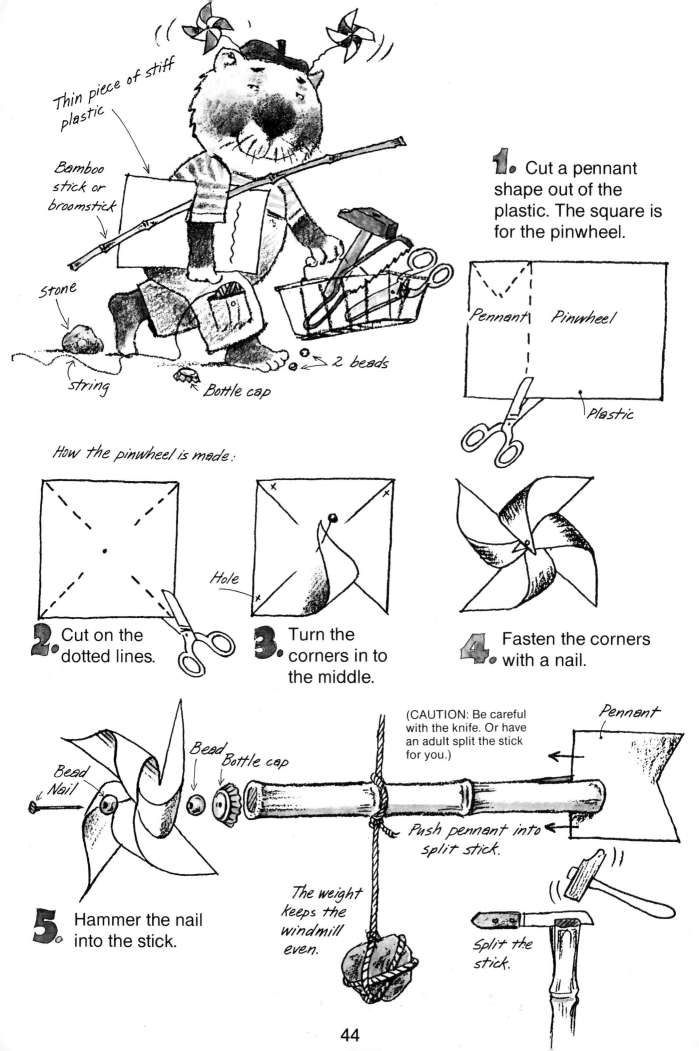

Thin piece of stiff plastic

Bamboo stick or broomstick

Stone

string

Bottle cap

2 beads

1. Cut a pennant shape out of the plastic. The square is for the pinwheel.

Pennant Pinwheel

Plastic

How the pinwheel is made:

2. Cut on the dotted lines.

3. Turn the corners in to the middle.

Hole

4. Fasten the corners with a nail.

Bead Nail

Bead

Bottle cap

5. Hammer the nail into the stick.

The weight keeps the windmill even.

(CAUTION: Be careful with the knife. Or have an adult split the stick for you.)

Pennant

Push pennant into split stick.

Split the stick.

Windmill

When the wind moves the plastic wings, the flag moves in a new direction. The sound is like the soft chirping of a cricket.

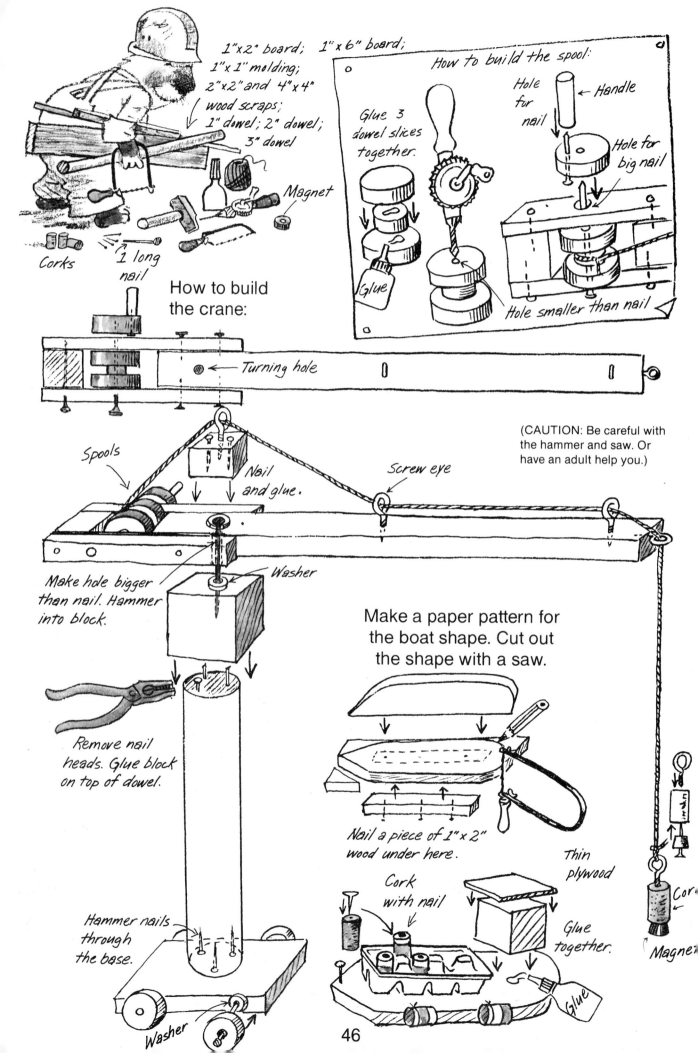

1"x2" board; 1"x6" board; 1"x 1" molding; 2"x2" and 4"x4" wood scraps; 1" dowel; 2" dowel; 3" dowel

Magnet

Corks

1 long nail

How to build the crane:

How to build the spool:

Handle

Hole for nail

Glue 3 dowel slices together.

Hole for big nail

Glue

Hole smaller than nail

Turning hole

(CAUTION: Be careful with the hammer and saw. Or have an adult help you.)

Spools

Nail and glue.

Screw eye

Make hole bigger than nail. Hammer into block.

Washer

Make a paper pattern for the boat shape. Cut out the shape with a saw.

Remove nail heads. Glue block on top of dowel.

Nail a piece of 1" x 2" wood under here.

Thin plywood

Cork with nail

Glue together.

Cor

Magnet

Hammer nails through the base.

Washer

Barge and Crane

The crane lifts the freight
with a small magnet.

Deck paint and clear varnish

Wood file Rasp

Coping saw

Board

Sandpaper

1. Cut out the duck body with the coping saw. Or let a grown-up help you.

2. Smooth the edges of the duck head with a rasp.

3. File one end of a dowel for the beak.

4. Glue on the head, the beak, and the tail.

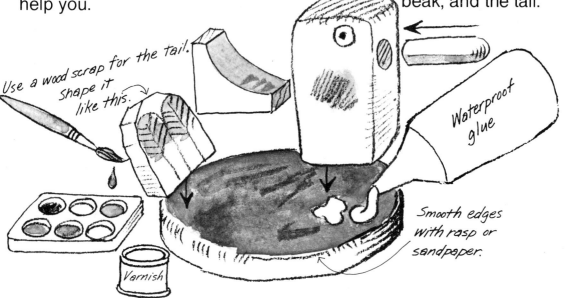

Use a wood scrap for the tail. Shape it like this.

Waterproof glue

Smooth edges with rasp or sandpaper.

Varnish

5. Paint the duck with deck paint and coat the feathers several times with clear varnish so that water can't wash the paint off.

Wooden Ducks

They rock around the pond
and meet for a "quack fest."

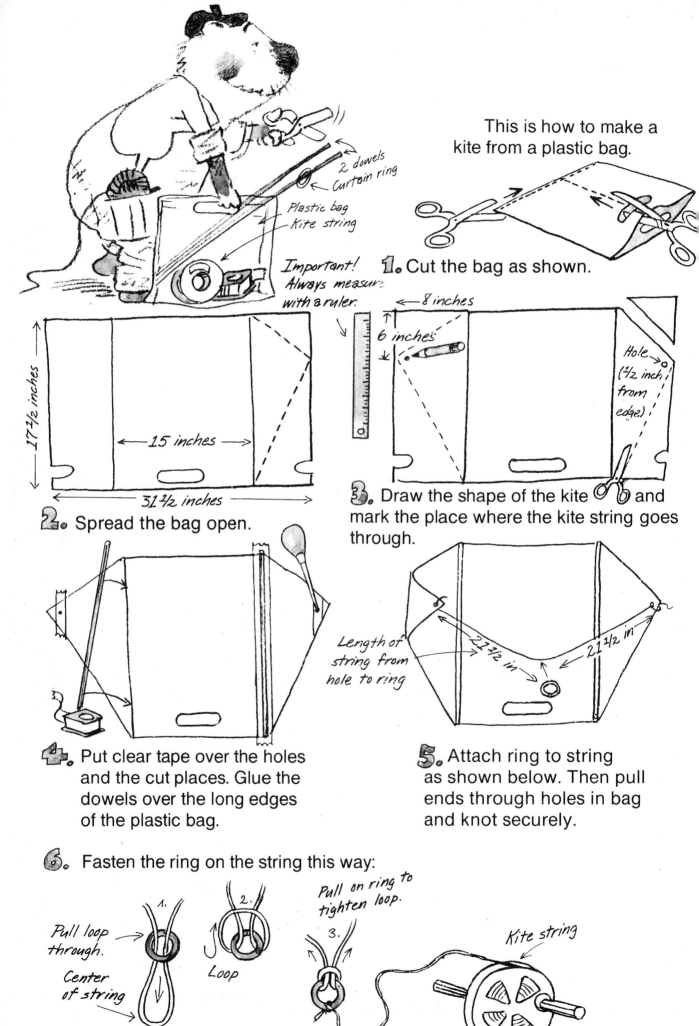

2 dowels
Curtain ring
Plastic bag
Kite string

This is how to make a kite from a plastic bag.

Important! Always measure with a ruler.

1. Cut the bag as shown.

17½ inches

15 inches

31½ inches

2. Spread the bag open.

← 8 inches
6 inches
Hole (½ inch from edge)

3. Draw the shape of the kite and mark the place where the kite string goes through.

Length of string from hole to ring

21½ in   21½ in

4. Put clear tape over the holes and the cut places. Glue the dowels over the long edges of the plastic bag.

5. Attach ring to string as shown below. Then pull ends through holes in bag and knot securely.

6. Fasten the ring on the string this way:

1.   2.   Pull on ring to tighten loop.

Pull loop through.

Center of string

Loop

3.

Kite string

Flying Bags

They climb high into the air
at the slightest breeze.

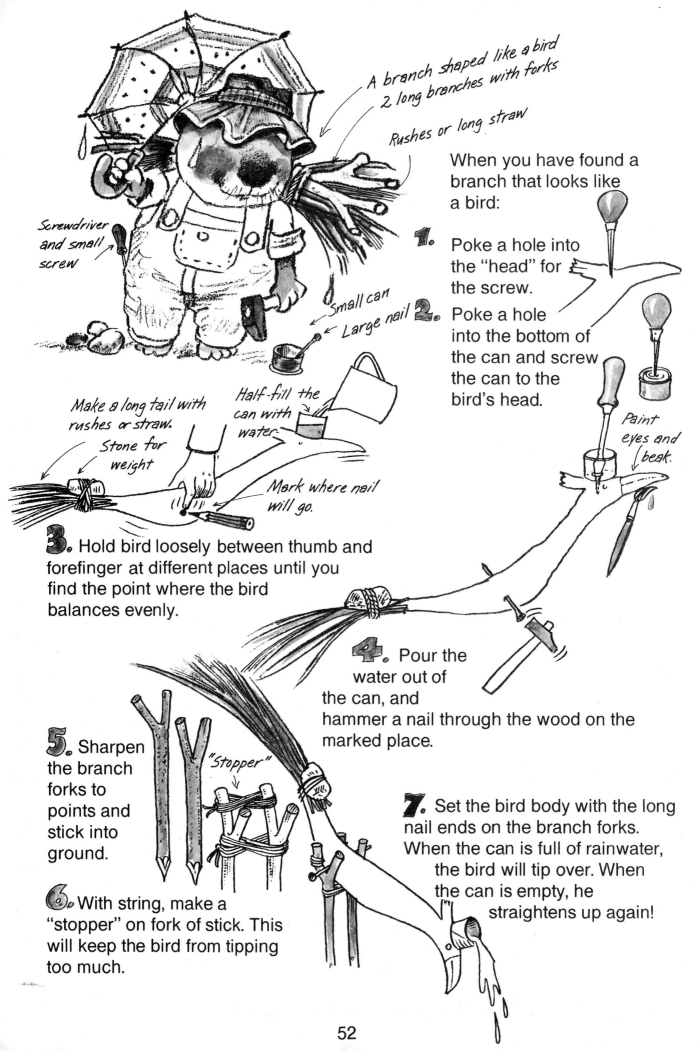

A branch shaped like a bird

2 long branches with forks

Rushes or long straw

Screwdriver and small screw

Small can

Large nail

When you have found a branch that looks like a bird:

1. Poke a hole into the "head" for the screw.

2. Poke a hole into the bottom of the can and screw the can to the bird's head.

Paint eyes and beak.

Make a long tail with rushes or straw.

Stone for weight

Half-fill the can with water.

Mark where nail will go.

3. Hold bird loosely between thumb and forefinger at different places until you find the point where the bird balances evenly.

4. Pour the water out of the can, and hammer a nail through the wood on the marked place.

5. Sharpen the branch forks to points and stick into ground.

"Stopper"

7. Set the bird body with the long nail ends on the branch forks. When the can is full of rainwater, the bird will tip over. When the can is empty, he straightens up again!

6. With string, make a "stopper" on fork of stick. This will keep the bird from tipping too much.

Rainbird

He struts through the reeds with
his long legs. He listens to the
wind. Will it bring rain?

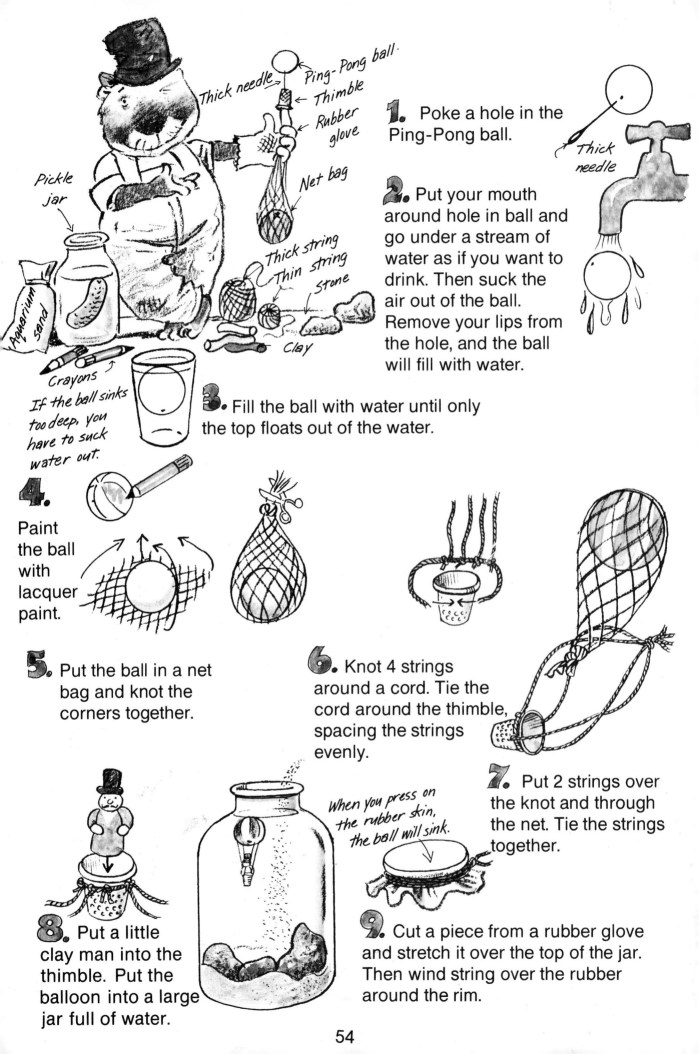

Thick needle → Ping-Pong ball
← Thimble
← Rubber glove
Net bag

Pickle jar

Aquarium sand

Thick string
Thin string
Stone

Clay

Crayons
If the ball sinks too deep, you have to suck water out.

1. Poke a hole in the Ping-Pong ball.

Thick needle

2. Put your mouth around hole in ball and go under a stream of water as if you want to drink. Then suck the air out of the ball. Remove your lips from the hole, and the ball will fill with water.

3. Fill the ball with water until only the top floats out of the water.

4. Paint the ball with lacquer paint.

5. Put the ball in a net bag and knot the corners together.

6. Knot 4 strings around a cord. Tie the cord around the thimble, spacing the strings evenly.

7. Put 2 strings over the knot and through the net. Tie the strings together.

When you press on the rubber skin, the ball will sink.

8. Put a little clay man into the thimble. Put the balloon into a large jar full of water.

9. Cut a piece from a rubber glove and stretch it over the top of the jar. Then wind string over the rubber around the rim.

Bottle Balloon

Mr. Roberts loves to fly up
and down in his balloon. He
lands in soft desert sand.

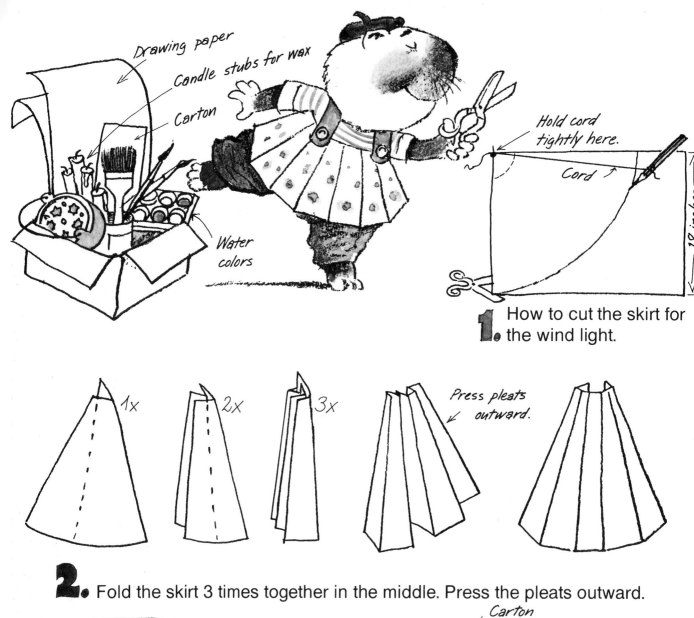

Drawing paper

Candle stubs for wax

Carton

Water colors

Hold cord tightly here.

Cord

18 inches

1. How to cut the skirt for the wind light.

1x   2x   3x

Press pleats outward.

2. Fold the skirt 3 times together in the middle. Press the pleats outward.

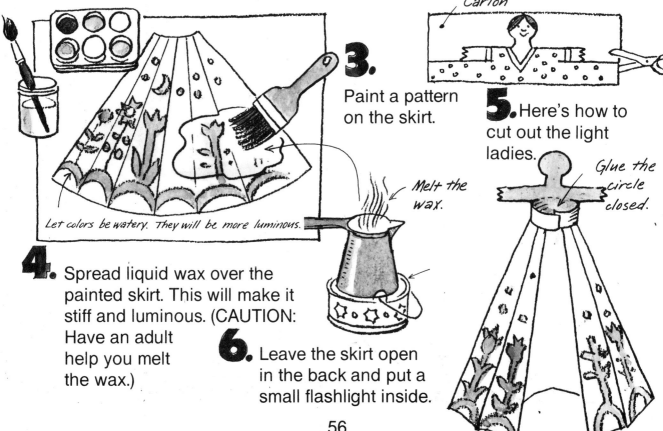

3. Paint a pattern on the skirt.

Let colors be watery. They will be more luminous.

Melt the wax.

4. Spread liquid wax over the painted skirt. This will make it stiff and luminous. (CAUTION: Have an adult help you melt the wax.)

Carton

5. Here's how to cut out the light ladies.

Glue the circle closed.

6. Leave the skirt open in the back and put a small flashlight inside.

Light Ladies

After the sun has dropped
behind the trees, the Light
Ladies will dance in the fields.

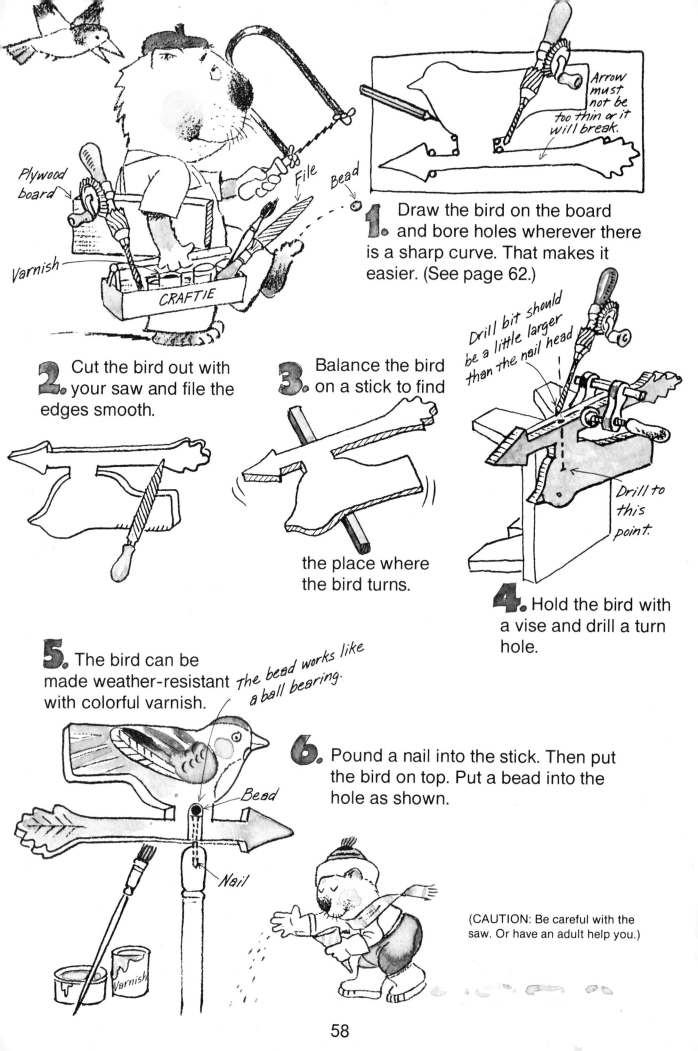

Plywood board

Varnish

File

Bead

CRAFTIE

Arrow must not be too thin or it will break.

1. Draw the bird on the board and bore holes wherever there is a sharp curve. That makes it easier. (See page 62.)

2. Cut the bird out with your saw and file the edges smooth.

3. Balance the bird on a stick to find the place where the bird turns.

Drill bit should be a little larger than the nail head

Drill to this point.

4. Hold the bird with a vise and drill a turn hole.

5. The bird can be made weather-resistant with colorful varnish.

The bead works like a ball bearing.

6. Pound a nail into the stick. Then put the bird on top. Put a bead into the hole as shown.

Bead

Nail

Varnish

(CAUTION: Be careful with the saw. Or have an adult help you.)

Snowbird

The snowbird will not fly away in the autumn.
Even in the winter, this bird will sit on his pole
and show which way the wind is blowing.

Wine glasses

Toothpicks

Glue

Clear tape

Tissue paper (red, pink, and yellow)

1. Take a strip of tissue paper that is wider than the height of your wine glasses. Make cuts for the flower petals.

Toothpick

Wet the point a bit.

2. Roll the corners with help of a toothpick.

Glue

3. Make little pleats in the bottom of each petal and glue together.

4. Fasten the strip with clear tape on the outside of the glass.

Put a small flashlight inside to light up your tulip.

Glue the end.

END

5. Wrap green tissue paper around stems of glasses.

60

Snow Tulips

On a snowy winter's night, your
snow tulips glow in window boxes.

I will show you the rules for using a coping saw.

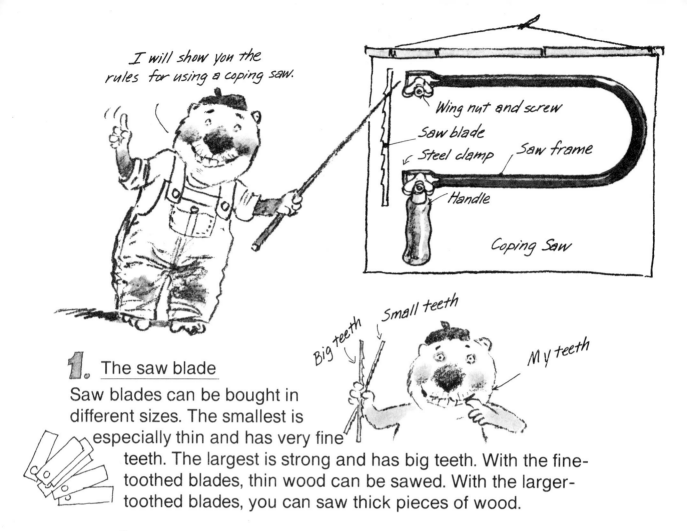

Wing nut and screw
Saw blade
Steel clamp
Saw frame
Handle

Coping Saw

1. The saw blade

Big teeth   Small teeth   My teeth

Saw blades can be bought in different sizes. The smallest is especially thin and has very fine teeth. The largest is strong and has big teeth. With the fine-toothed blades, thin wood can be sawed. With the larger-toothed blades, you can saw thick pieces of wood.

A too-thin saw blade will break quickly if you saw thick wood.

Remember:
A strong wood needs a strong saw blade!

A too-thick saw blade will rip thin wood and make frayed-looking cuts.

2. The inserting of blades

It is important that the teeth of the blade go *down* and *outward* when you insert it in the saw frame.

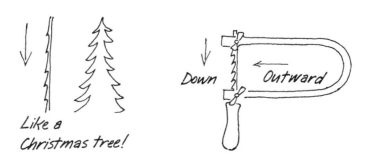

Like a Christmas tree!

Down   Outward

62

Put one end of the saw blade into the top clamp (saw side out). Screw the wing nut tight. Then put the bottom end of the blade into the bottom clamp. Before you tighten the saw blade on the bottom, the frame has to be pushed together a bit so that the blade will be taut.

. Sawing

Plywood is best for use with a coping saw. You can buy it 1/8-in. thick to 5/8-in. thick. Put the wood on a table for sawing. Fasten the wood to the table with a clamp. So that the table will not be damaged, hold the board in one hand. *Pull* the sawing blade to saw, *don't push forward.*

Clamp

When pushing the saw up, tilt it slightly back. If you pull the teeth of a saw blade through a piece of soap occasionally, the sawing goes very smoothly, and the blade does not rip the wood so easily. When going around a sharp corner, do not turn the saw into the new direction, or the blade will tear the wood. First saw up and down several times in one place. Then turn the blade very slowly in the new direction. With thicker wood, it is easier to go around corners if you drill holes at the corners before you saw.

Drill holes to turn corners.

Take the blade out of the frame after sawing. With a set of pliers, you can turn the blade easily.

So long! Have fun! And don't cut your fingers!

Your friend, Craftie

INDEX